# INSIDE...

Page **6**

GODS AND MONSTERS!

Page **22**

TO SAVE TOMORROW!

Page **36** THE RULE OF FOUR!

BATTLE STATIONS!

Page **49**

£7.99

A copy of the comic he first appeared in (Amazing Fantasy #15) sold for $227,000!

Before fighting crime, he tried pro wrestling to make money!

He's about 15 times more agile than a regular human!

Peter Parker is actually scared of heights!

Any part of his body can cling to walls, not just his hands and feet!

He can make rafts, hang-gliders and skis with his webbing!

Nothing can prise him away from walls he wants to cling to!

He once grew 4 extra arms when he tried to get rid of his powers!

He once drove a Spidey-Mobile, with two built-in web cannons!

# SPIDER-MAN™
# FACT ATTACK

US President, Barack Obama, has featured on the cover of Amazing Spider-Man!

His webshooters are made of plastic, to avoid metal detectors!

His first ever battle was against the Chameleon!

A Spider-Man musical came to Broadway in 2010!

He once wore a steel-plated costume to battle the New Enforcers!

He's fought monsters like the Mummy, Frankenstein's Monster and Dracula!

His Aunt May was almost married to Doc Ock!

MY SPIDER SENSE IS TELLING ME ONE OF THESE FACTS IS FALSE! FIND OUT WHICH ONE ON PAGE 62!

5

YOU KNOW, FROSTY, I WAS LOOKING FOR ICE-CREAM. DON'T SUPPOSE YOU'VE GOT A TUB OF COCONUT--

UNGH!

CEASE YOUR PRATTLE MORTAL!

SWAKK

OUCH, THAT HURT!

BUT IF I DON'T DO SOMETHING, THAT COP'S HAD IT!

HRRRRr!

PNUT! PNUT!

GET BACK! GET BACK!!!

GOTTA TELL YA, FUZZY, THAT LORD OF THE RINGS LOOK IS SO LAST YEAR!

SPIDEY! I THOUGHT I WAS A GONER THERE!

LISTEN GUYS, THESE BOZOS ARE WAY OUT OF YOUR LEAGUE --

YOU'VE GOT TO FALL BACK AND LET THE AVENGERS HANDLE THEM.

FORGET IT, SPIDER-MAN,

THEY'RE OFF ON SOME OUTER-SPACE MISSION WITH THE FANTASTIC FOUR --

THE CITY'S DEFENCELESS!

...CONSIDERING I'M ABOUT SEVEN SECONDS AWAY FROM GETTING SQUISHED!

SEIZE HIM!

GRIND H BONES!

NO IT ISN'T, NOT WHILE I'M STILL IN ACTION!

SAY, THAT SOUNDED GOOD...

CONTINUED ON PAGE 12

# SPIDER FILE: THOR ™

He is a god who walks the Earth, Lord of the Living Lightning and heir to the throne of Asgard! Read on, web heads, to learn more about the mighty THOR!

## SPIDEY DATA:

REAL NAME: THOR
OCCUPATION: MEMBER OF THE AVENGERS AND RULER OF ASGARD
HEIGHT: 6' 6"
WEIGHT: 640 LBS
EYE COLOUR: BLUE
HAIR COLOUR: BLONDE
BASE OF OPERATIONS: AVENGERS MANSION / ASGARD
POWERS / ABILITIES: INCREDIBLE COMBAT SKILLS AND SUPERHUMAN LEVELS OF STRENGTH AND TOUGHNESS.

STRENGTH:

AGILITY:

INTELLIGENCE:

SPEED:

FIGHTING SKILL:

"BACK, YON VILLAIN -- OR FACE THE POWER OF THE MIGHTY MJOLINOR!"

His skin is so tough conventional weapons cannot pierce it!

He can fly through the air by throwing his Hammer and holding on to its leather handle! Traveling like this, he can achieve speeds of up to 2000 mph!

FIRST APPEARANCE: JOURNEY INTO MYSTERY #83 (1962)

When wearing his enchanted belt of strength, Thor can easily lift up to 200 tons!

# GLORY OF THE GODS!

Raised in the mystical kingdom of Asgard, Thor is the son of the Norse God Odin. By the age of sixteen, he had already saved his homeland from a slew of dragons, trolls and giants, and had gained a reputation as a mighty warrior. Unfortunately, this fame had also caused him to become arrogant and incredibly headstrong.

# A MORTAL LIFE!

In order to teach him a lesson in humility, Odin banished Thor to the mortal world and made him live his life as a crippled surgeon called Donald Blake, unaware of his real identity. After ten years Odin revealed to Thor his true nature and invited him to return to Asgard.

# DIVINE CHAMPION!

But Thor had grown attached to the world of humans and decided not to return to Asgard permanently. He now splits his time between his mystical home and the mortal world, where he uses his god-like abilities to smite the unjust and protect the innocent.

# THE SECRETS OF MJOLNIR!

Forged from the mystical metal URU, Thor's hammer is nearly indestructible. Its powers are further boosted by five incredible enchantments!

**1.** Only a person who is worthy of the gods can lift the hammer of Thor.

**2.** After striking its target, the hammer will always return to the hand of the person who threw it.

**3.** It can be used to control the weather; summoning immense storms and gales, or firing bolts of lightning!

**4.** Thor can use the hammer to open interdimensional portals so he can travel between Earth and Asgard!

**5.** The fifth enchantment enables Thor to change between his god-like appearance and that of Donald Blake. Thor rarely uses this ability any more as he prefers to stay in his divine form.

11

CONTINUED ON PAGE 17

# LOKI

Loki is Thor's half-brother and the Norse God of Lies. Or is he? Read on to find out the twisted truth about this deceiving deity!

## BITTER RIVALS!

Adopted by Lord Odin after his father Laufey the frost giant was killed in battle, Loki was raised in the Asgardian royal court. Even from a young age he was insanely jealous of his half-brother Thor's abilities, and would spend hours plotting schemes to kill him.

## DARK ARTS!

As he grew older, Loki discovered he had a natural gift for magic and began studying the mystic arts. He hoped to use his new magical abilities to destroy his step-brother and claim the throne of Asgard for himself.

His magical knowledge gives him loads of extra powers including energy projection, teleportation, and flight!

## ACT OF GODS!

Though he has personally attacked Thor in the past, Loki prefers to use other people as pawns in his plans, usually controlling them with magic or deceiving them with a web of lies. Though Thor has managed to stop him in the past, Loki will not cease his plans until he is crowned king of Asgard!

By using his powers of hypnotism and illusion casting, he can twist people's perceptions to make them believe nearly anything!

Though he is weak for an Asgardian, he is still much stronger than a normal human and can lift nearly 30 tons!

Loki is responsible for the creation of Crusher Creel AKA The Absorbing Man. He granted Crusher the power to change his body into whatever he touches in the hope that he would become strong enough to defeat Thor!

CONTINUED FROM PAGE 15

17

AND WHAT OF OUR TREASURES? OUR PRECIOUS GEMS AND JEWELS?

FEAR NOT, STORM GIANT. RETURN THEE TO THINE REALMS AND ALL WILL BE RESTORED --

SO SAYETH THOR!

AND SO...

THAT'S REALLY IT THEN?

AYE, SPIDER-MAN. AND KNOW THOU THIS...

...BY PROTECTING YON MAIDEN, THOU HATH SHOWN THYSELF TO BE AMONGST THE BRAVEST OF THY MORTAL RACE.

AW, SHUCKS.

NOW, COMRADE, I MUST MAKE FOR ASGARD --

WHERE LOKI SHALL TASTE THE WRATHFUL JUSTICE OF ODIN, THE ALL-FATHER!

FWASH

YEP, AND I'VE GOTTA BE RUNNING ALONG TOO.

LATERS, RED.

EPILOGUE, THAT EVENING

...I STILL CAN'T BELIEVE YOU GAVE HARRY THE SLIP AND CAME AFTER ME, MJ --

YOU COULD HAVE GOTTEN HURT, OR WORSE.

SORRY, TIGER, I GUESS I PANICKED WHEN I COULDN'T FIND YOU.

BUT GET THIS, WHEN THINGS GOT SCARY...

...I STARTED GETTING THIS WEIRD FEELING,

LIKE YOU WERE NEARBY AND TRYING TO PROTECT ME.

HONEY, YOU'D BETTER BELIEVE IT.

THE END. VERILY.

19

# SECRETS OF ASGARD!

Hey, web heads! Wanna get the lowdown on Thor's homeland of Asgard? Read on to find out more!

## GODS OF ASGARD!

Thor is a member of a race called the Aesir. These guys may look like humans but take it from me; you don't want to challenge one to an arm-wrestling contest. They're way stronger than normal humans and can easily lift around 25 tons without breaking a sweat, plus they can live for thousands of years! Just to make them even harder, they're totally impervious to all human diseases. (So that's why you never see Thor with a hankie!)

## THE ALL-FATHER!

The Aesir are ruled by Thor's father **Odin**. Odin is a wise king and a mighty warrior. His vast knowledge is mainly thanks to his two ravens **Huginn** and **Muninn**, who travel the world collecting information. However, these aren't the only weird pets he owns. He also has two pet wolves called **Geri** and **Freki** and an eight-legged horse called **Hlidskjalf**! In battle he wields a magical spear that has been enchanted so that it never misses its target.

## ANCIENT KNOWLEDGE!

Odin is one guy you do not want to mess with. In order to learn how to make magical markings called runes he once had to hang himself upside down from a tree for nine days without food or water! Now that's dedication!

## CROSSING THE VOID!

Although there are a few naturally existing portals between Asgard and the Earth, they are hard to find and are often in very inhospitable areas. To make it easier for Asgardians to travel to Earth, Odin created a rainbow bridge called Bifrost connecting the two worlds.

## NONE SHALL PASS!

The bridge is guarded by the mighty warrior Heimdall who will not let anybody pass unless they have permission from Odin.

# LAND OF THE GIANTS!

The giants of Asgard live in a place called **Jotunheim**. These guys are normally about thirty feet tall and are famous for their bad temper! (Probably cos they can never find shoes in their size!) There are two different types of giants, **Storm Giants** who live in the mountains, and **Frost Giants** who live in the frozen wasteland.

## FAFNIR! THE STORM GIANT

Like all Storm giants, Fafnir is huge in size and strength. He can also control the elements and summon mighty storms and high winds.

Ymir is the oldest of the Frost giants and easily the most powerful. He can lift over 100 tons and his dense icy skin makes him nearly impossible to injure. He can generate immense cold from his body and is able to freeze anything he touches!

## YMIR! THE FROST GIANT

According to the Norse Gods' legends, Asgard exists within the roots of a giant tree called Ygdrasil. (They'd better keep an eye out for giant squirrels then! — Ed.)

Though not as large as the giants, trolls are still powerfully built creatures normally standing at about 8 feet tall. They are more intelligent than giants and are incredibly sneaky.

## TROLLS!

Just to make living there even more dangerous, Asgard is also home to loads of giant fire-breathing **dragons**!

## WARRIORS OF ASGARD!

Thor isn't the only Asgardian to become a Super Hero. His childhood sweetheart Sif and Brunhilde the Valkyrie have also journeyed to Earth in order to protect human kind.

Another of the races who live in Asgard are the Dwarves. They are shorter than the Aesir and live in a region called Nidavellir. They have a natural talent for engineering and are highly skilled craftsmen. They created many of Asgard's most famous treasures, including Thor's hammer and Odin's spear.

RECORDING. PERSONAL LOG. 11.34 PM, AUGUST 1ST, 2005. NEW YORK CITY.

IN THE DISTANCE, I CAN SEE MY TARGET. THE BAXTER BUILDING - HOME TO THE FANTASTIC FOUR.

I AM CLOSE NOW. IT HAS TAKEN YEARS OF PAIN AND SACRIFICE TO BRING ME TO THIS PLACE.

BUT TONIGHT, AT LAST, IT WILL ALL BE WORTH IT.

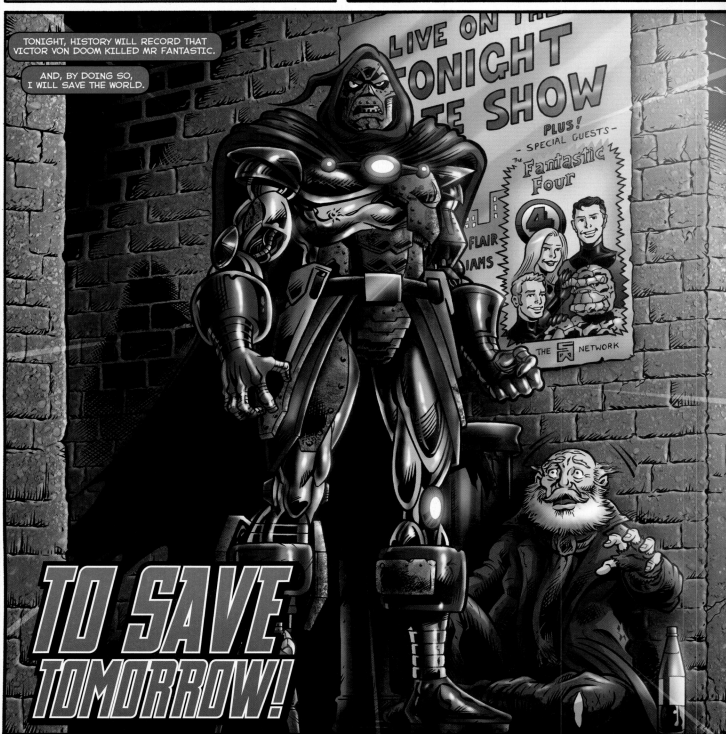

TONIGHT, HISTORY WILL RECORD THAT VICTOR VON DOOM KILLED MR FANTASTIC.

AND, BY DOING SO, I WILL SAVE THE WORLD.

LIVE ON THE TONIGHT LATE SHOW

PLUS! - SPECIAL GUESTS -

The Fantastic Four

THE NETWORK

# TO SAVE TOMORROW!

SCRIPT: MITCHEL SCANLON PENCILS: SIMON WILLIAMS INKS: SIMON ECOB COLOURS: JASON CARDY LETTERS: NEIL PORTER

AND THEN, THERE WAS ONE.

YOUR TEAMMATES ARE DEFEATED, SUSAN RICHARDS. BUT MY ORIGINAL OFFER STILL STANDS. SURRENDER NOW AND-

GONE..?

OF COURSE, I SHOULD HAVE SUSPECTED YOU WOULD RENDER YOURSELF AND YOUR HUSBAND INVISIBLE TO TRY TO ELUDE ME.

CLEVER, SUSAN. BUT ULTIMATELY POINTLESS.

IT IS A SIMPLE MATTER TO ADJUST MY ARMOUR'S SCANNING SYSTEMS TO VIEW OTHER PARTS OF THE SPECTRUM AND THEN...

KLIK

'AH. THERE YOU ARE.'

YOU CAN MAKE ALL THE OFFERS YOU WANT, DOOM. I'M NOT GOING TO LET YOU HURT MY HUSBAND!

A NOBLE SENTIMENT, SUSAN...

SADLY, NOT ONE THAT IS WITHIN YOUR POWER TO SEE REALISED.

UHHH—

ZZLOWWWW!

AND SO IT ENDS. YOU ARE HELPLESS, REED RICHARDS. UNCONSCIOUS.

AFTER SO MANY YEARS OF ENMITY, IT SEEMS ALMOST WRONG TO KILL YOU LIKE THIS...

25

IT'S CLOBBERIN' TIME!

WHOOOMPPP!!

KRAKKKK!!!

NICE WORK, WEBHEAD, KEEPIN' TALL, DARK AND GRUESOME HERE BUSY 'TIL WE WUZ BACK ON OUR FEET.

HEY! WATCH IT! HE'S GETTING UP AGAIN!

CALM YOURSELF, JONATHAN STORM. YOU HAVE NO NEED FOR ALARM.

IF WHAT SPIDER-MAN TOLD ME EARLIER IS TRUE, THEN OUR BATTLE HERE IS ENDED.

ENDED, HUH? JUST LIKE THAT? YER MASK MUST BE ON TOO TIGHT, DOOM, IF YA THINK WE'RE GONNA FALL FER TH-

WAIT, BEN! LET'S HEAR HIM OUT.

STRETCH?! FER A MINUTE THERE, I THOUGHT YA WUZ A GONER...

I'M FINE, BEN. ALL THE SAME THOUGH, I WANT SOME ANSWERS.

CONTINUED ON PAGE 29

27

# SPIDER-MAN TRUTH TRAIL

Heads up, Spidey fans! The Green Goblin has kidnapped Mary Jane and I need to get through this maze to find her! Each time you reach a box you need to decide whether the statement is true or false and follow that path. But be careful, guys, if you take the wrong path I'm gonna end up in the clutches of one of these super villains!

**START**

Spider-Man's real name is Peter Parker

FALSE / TRUE

Doctor Octopus has 10 robotic arms

TRUE / FALSE

The Green Goblin's real name is Norman Osborn

FALSE / TRUE

Spider-Man lives in New York

TRUE / FALSE

Aunt May is really the Sandman.

TRUE / FALSE

**FINISH**

The Vulture has a blue costume

FALSE / TRUE

**ANSWERS ON PAGE 62...**

28

# FANTASTIC FOUR

## NAME: THE FANTASTIC FOUR

**MR FANTASTIC**
REED RICHARDS

**THE INVISIBLE WOMAN**
SUE RICHARDS

**THE HUMAN TORCH**
JOHNNY STORM

**THE THING**
BEN GRIMM

**BASE OF OPERATIONS:** THE BAXTER BUILDING, NEW YORK.
**ORIGIN OF POWERS:** CONTACT WITH COSMIC PARTICLES

WANNA KNOW HOW THE FANTASTIC FOURSOME GOT THEIR POWERS, WEB HEADS? JUST READ ON TO FIND OUT!

### ONE MAN'S DREAM!

Reed Richard's greatest ambition was to create a spaceship capable of interstellar flight. Working with the U.S. government Reed spent years researching and building his dream project. However, disaster struck when the project was closed down days before the first test flight!

### TO REACH THE STARS!

Determined to fulfil his dream, Reed, along with his fiancée Sue, her brother Johnny and his best friend Ben Grimm, broke into the military base and stole the experimental ship!

### CALM BEFORE THE STORM!

Soaring through the night sky, all seemed to go well with the first unplanned test-flight until they left the safety of the Earth's atmosphere.

# COSMIC CALAMITY!

Without warning they were bombarded by a wave of cosmic particles that ripped through the ship's weak shielding! Damaged and out of control, the crippled ship tumbled back towards the Earth!

# AN AMAZING TRANSFORMATION!

After a bumpy landing, the four crawled from the wreckage of the ship and made a shocking discovery. The cosmic rays had granted each of them fantastic powers! Reed discovered he could stretch his body like rubber, Sue somehow had the power to turn invisible, Johnny could transform his entire body into living flame and Ben Grimm found his skin had changed into an almost unbreakable rock-like substance!

# POWER AND RESPONSIBILITY!

Realising they now possessed more power than any human on the planet, they took a vow to use their abilities to protect the world. As Earth's first family of super heroes they set up base atop the Baxter Building in New York and renamed themselves the Fantastic Four!

NOT WANTING TO COMPLAIN, BUT YOU KNOW BEING "THE AMAZING SPIDER-MAN" COMES WITH MORE THAN ITS SHARE OF HEADACHES.

TAKE RIGHT NOW, FOR EXAMPLE. HERE'S YOURS TRULY, RIDING IN THE FANTASTICAR WITH THE FF AND DOC DOOM — ALL OF US ON OUR WAY TO ANOTHER DIMENSION.

ZZZZZZOOOOOOM

AND IT ALL STARTED BECAUSE DOOM HERE SHOWED UP CLAIMING HE WASN'T THE DOC DOOM WE KNOW.

INSTEAD, HE SAYS HE'S FROM AN ALTERNATE EARTH — ONE WHERE HIS WORLD'S VERSION OF REED RICHARDS HAS GONE CRAZY AND TAKEN OVER THE PLANET.

SHEESH. YOU SEE WHAT I MEAN? ALTERNATE WORLDS. PARALLEL EARTHS. GOOD GUYS GONE BAD...

YOU GOT TO FIGURE IF I WAS PETER PARKER THE AMAZING ACCOUNTANT, I WOULDN'T HAVE TO DEAL WITH THESE KINDS OF PROBLEMS.

...ALMOST THERE. A FEW MORE SECONDS AND WE'LL KNOW WHETHER YOUR STORY IS TRUE, DOOM.

YOU STILL DOUBT ME, RICHARDS? VERY WELL...

LOOK NOW AND YOU WILL SEE PROOF OF EVERYTHING I TOLD YOU. LOOK, AND SEE HOW ONE MAN'S DREAM CAN BECOME A WHOLE WORLD'S NIGHTMARE...

HEROES FOREVER
THEY GAVE THEIR LIVES TO SAVE US

A STATUE TO BEN, JOHNNY AND ME? BUT WHY...

BECAUSE YOU ARE DEAD, SUSAN: ALL THREE OF YOU.

OR RATHER, HE ALTERNATE VERSIONS OF YOU THAT EXISTED IN THIS WORLD ARE DEAD. FIVE YEARS AGO, THEY GAVE THEIR LIVES TO DEFEAT AN ATTEMPTED ALIEN INVASION OF EARTH.

'BUT THOUGH WE WERE ALL CHANGED BY THAT INVASION, REED RICHARDS WAS CHANGED MOST OF ALL.

'DRIVEN MAD BY GRIEF, HE CREATED AN ARMY OF ROBOTS IN THE IMAGE OF HIS FALLEN TEAMMATES AND SEIZED CONTROL OF THE WORLD.'

40

BUT TONIGHT, HE WILL GO EVEN FARTHER. THESE HEADBANDS ARE RECEIVERS, DESIGNED TO PICK UP THE BROADCASTS OF A RECENTLY-LAUNCHED RING OF MIND-CONTROL SATELLITES.

WITH THEM, ONCE THE SYSTEM GOES ONLINE, REED RICHARDS WILL TURN THE ENTIRE POPULATION OF EARTH INTO HIS MINDLESS SLAVES.

THAT IS, UNLESS WE STOP HIM.

KRRMP

CONTINUED ON PAGE 42...

# 5 THINGS YOU NEVER KNEW ABOUT... DR. DOOM

Hey, web heads! Just in case you had forgotten how bad the Dr. Doom from our world really is, check out this selection of tyrannical trivia about the Latverian loony!

## 1. HUNGRY FOR POWER!

Doom's got a serious thing for stealing other people's abilities! He once managed to capture the Silver Surfer and harness his COSMIC POWER! However his greatest scoop was when he stole the powers of an omnipotent being called the Beyonder!

## 2. SORCEROUS WAYS!

Although he prefers to use scientific means to achieve his goals, Doom does have a small amount of magical power thanks to his mother who was a potent gypsy witch.

HOLY SMOKES! HE'S A ROBOT!

## 3. ROBO-DOOM

Doom has a loyal army of powerful DOOM-BOTS which have been programmed to believe that they are the real Dr. Doom unless they are in the presence of him or another Doom-bot. You won't believe the amount of times some Super Hero has clobbered Doom only to discover it was actually one of these mechanical mimics!

## 4. TAG-TEAM!

This isn't the first time Spidey has had to fight alongside Dr. Doom! They once teamed up to defeat a powerful being called the Dark Rider!

## 5. TERRIBLE TYRANT!

Along with being a power crazed super villain, Dr. Doom is also the king of the small Balkan nation of Latveria. He rules the country with an iron fist and harshly punishes anyone who disagrees with him!

CONTINUED FROM PAGE 40

THE BAXTER BUILDING...

ALL I WANTED WAS TO BUILD A PERFECT WORLD. A WORLD WITHOUT PAIN OR SADNESS...

...IS THAT REALLY SO HARD TO UNDERSTAND?

NO, OF COURSE NOT, REED.

THEN WHY ARE PEOPLE SO STUBBORN? DON'T THEY UNDERSTAND I'M ONLY TRYING TO HELP THEM?

MAYBE YOU JUST NEED TO TRY HARDER WITH THEM, REED.

YES. TRY HARDER. THAT'S WHERE THE MIND-CONTROL SATELLITES COME IN. ONCE I'VE ABOLISHED FREE WILL, THEN EVERYTHING WILL BE ALLRIGHT.

YOU ARE SO CLEVER, REED. I KNEW YOU WOULD FIND A SOLUTION.

WHY, THANK YOU, DARLING. YOU KNOW, SOMETIMES, I THINK YOU'RE THE ONLY ONE WHO REALLY UNDERSTANDS ME. OH, AND SUE?

42

YES, REED?

YES, REED

YOU SEEM TO HAVE FORGOTTEN TO PUT YOUR FACE ON THIS MORNING. FIX IT, PLEASE.

WAH-WAH-WEEEEE

THE INTRUDER ALARM? BUT THAT WOULD ONLY SOUND IF WE WERE UNDER ATT--

KRR-KRMMPP

I DON'T GET IT. HE REALISES WE AIN'T ROBOTS AND THE FIGHT GOES OUTTA HIM?

DON'T YOU SEE, BEN? KILLING US WOULD'VE BEEN LIKE LOSING HIS TEAMMATES ALL OVER AGAIN. IT WAS TOO MUCH FOR HIM TO TAKE.

NOT WANTING TO INTERRUPT, GUYS.

BUT WITH DOOM HEADED FOR THAT CONTROL PANEL, ANYBODY ELSE HAVE THE SNEAKING SUSPICION HE'S ABOUT TO REVERT TO TYPE?

SATELLITE MASTER CONTROL

YOU NEEDN'T WORRY, SPIDER-MAN. SUCH SUSPICIONS ARE ENTIRELY GROUNDLESS.

SHRAZ

I TOLD YOU WE WERE ALL CHANGED BY THE ALIEN INVASION.

GRANTED, THERE WAS ONCE A TIME WHEN I DREAMED OF RULING THE WORLD...

46

'UNTIL I SAW WHERE SUCH DREAMS CAN LEAD A MAN.

I ONLY WANTED TO MAKE THINGS BETTER...

I ONLY WANTED TO MAKE THINGS BETTER...

'NOW GO, ALL OF YOU. GO, SAFE IN THE KNOWLEDGE THERE WILL BE NO MORE TYRANNY ON THIS PLANET.

FWOOOOOOSHHHH

'ON THAT, YOU HAVE MY WORD.'

BUT THAT'S JUST IT, JOHNNY. WE FACE CHOICES THROUGHOUT OUR LIVES.

IN THE END, WE HAVE TO STICK TO WHAT WE KNOW IS RIGHT....

YOU KNOW, IT'S SPOOKY. I MEAN, THE REED OF THIS WORLD STARTED OUT WITH SUCH GOOD INTENTIONS.

THEN HE MADE SOME BAD CHOICES AND LOOK WHERE IT LED HIM.

'AND, AFTER THAT, ALL WE CAN DO IS HOPE FOR BEST.'

HEROES FOREVER
THEY GAVE THEIR LIVES TO SAVE US

THE END

47

# FANTASTIC FOES!

The Fantastic Four have saved the world from hundreds of super powered villains. See if you can find the names of their most famous foes in this giant sized word grid!

```
A M Y U M Y X Y E R I O P K
N A M E L U C E L O M A L D
N P S Y C H O M A N H A I F
I A Z L S Z R R R A W K M M
H S D L U D D O D N E N P O
I R F S P F O R W Y M O O D
L E A E E A O L E A L S S U
U T M D R D O O M B T U S L
S S C E S C A R A L T W I U
N A L N K L B I D A O H B S
R M A R R A D M T S B I L S
B T A B U A V B H T Z A E D
U E L E L L D P I A H N M F
L P Z L L Z R R N A C A A H
L P D L S B D O K R E M N U
S U F S T F I R E Y U E X T
E P A E A A O C R A A L N E
Y F R I G H T F U L F O U R
E A C E A C A R L R T M A R
G A L A C T U S G B C H C A
R R A T E R M I N U S I U X
```

BULLSEYE
DR DOOM
DIABLO
KLAW
GALACTUS
RONAN

SUPERSKRULL
IMPOSSIBLE MAN
PUPPET MASTER
MAD THINKER
MOLECULE MAN
PSYCHO-MAN
FRIGHTFUL FOUR
MOLE MAN
ANNIHILUS
BLASTAAR
CRUCIBLE
MODULUS
TERMINUS
TERRAX

ANSWERS ON PAGE 62...

HE'S GOT INCREDIBLE STRENGTH AND AGILITY. HE CAN SPIN A WEB AND SCALE EVEN THE TALLEST OF BUILDINGS. BUT TODAY, IN SPITE OF ALL THESE POWERS, THE AMAZING SPIDER-MAN IS...

...BORED STUPID, MAN!

I MEAN, NEW YORK'S NORMALLY CRAWLING WITH CRIMINALS AND SUPER VILLAINS -- BUT I'VE BEEN PATROLLING FOR HOURS NOW AND ZIP. TOTAL ZIP.

IN FACT, RIGHT NOW I'D EVEN SETTLE FOR A FEW ROUNDS WITH FROG-MAN. SAD OR WHAT?

# BATTLE STATIONS!

SCRIPT: FERG HANDLEY
PENCILS: SIMON WILLIAMS
INKS: SIMON ECOB
COLOURS: JASON CARDY
LETTERING: ED HAMMOND & ANDY LENG

HOLD ON THOUGH.

SQUAD CARS. SIRENS. BLUE LIGHTS.

SO WHAT AM I WAITING FOR?!

WOOOW WOOOW

MANHATTAN'S FIFTH AVENUE, LOCATION OF...

...AVENGERS MANSION?!

SAY, OFFICER, WHAT'S THE LOWDOWN HERE? ALIEN INVASION? KILLER ROBOTS? SPACE MONKEYS?

HARD TO SAY, SPIDER-MAN. THE BUILDING'S COMMUNICATION LINKS ARE DOWN AND THERE'S BEEN EXPLOSIONS REPORTED INSIDE --

APART FROM THAT, WE'RE IN THE DARK.

49

WAIT A MINUTE, OVER BY THAT WINDOW. LOOKS LIKE BOOMERANG AND THE HOBGOBLIN!

"YEAH, THAT'S THEM ALRIGHT. MAYBE WE GOT A NEW VERSION OF THE SINISTER SIX IN TOWN..."

"...THOUGH WHY THEY'D BE ATTACKING THE AVENGERS AND NOT ME IS A MITE PUZZLING."

STILL, THOSE TWO ARE MY ENEMIES, SO I'D BETTER CHECK IT OUT. BESIDES, CAP AND THE GANG HAVE HELPED ME OUT IN THE PAST, I GUESS I OWE THEM ONE.

AND SO...

ALARMS SYSTEMS ARE ALL DOWN, SO GETTING IN WAS A BREEZE. BUT WHERE'S THE AVENGERS... AND WHAT CAUSED ALL THIS DAMAGE?

WHOA, THAT NOISE -- SOUNDS LIKE SOME SORT OF HEAVY DUTY ENGINE.

VRRRRR

THE MANSION'S HANGAR BAY...

IT'S AN AVENGERS QUINJET TAKING OFF...AND I'M TOO LATE TO STOP IT!

VRRRROOM

OKAY, WEBHEAD, CONCENTRATE. WHAT WOULD THE HOBGOBLIN WANT WITH --

-- WHOA!

EASY, BUDDY, I'M ON YOUR SIDE HERE!

SPIDER-MAN! SORRY, PAL, THOUGHT IT WAS ANOTHER OF THOSE PSYCHOS LURKING UP THERE.

THAT'S RIGHT, MISTER! NOW GET DOWN HERE BEFORE I REALLY CUT LOOSE -- AND DON'T TRY ANYTHING STUPID!

HE FIRST CAME ON THE SCENE AS ANT-MAN, THEN LATER BECAME GIANT-MAN. BUT THESE DAYS, DOCTOR HANK PYM FIGHTS HIS BATTLES AS --

YELLOWJACKET!

SO, WHERE'S THE REST OF THE GANG, YJ?

THOR'S ON A LEAVE OF ABSENCE, WHILE THE VISION AND THE SCARLET WITCH ARE IN EUROPE ON A MISSION.

THE REST OF US WERE IN THE MAIN COMPUTER ROOM...

"...UPDATING FILES, WHEN A HOLE SUDDENLY OPENED UP IN THE FLOOR..."

WASP, HAWKEYE, BATTLE STATIONS! IRON MAN, SEE IF YOU CAN PICK ANYTHING UP ON YOUR SCANNERS!

ON IT, CAP.

"THEN, OUT OF THE SHAFT EMERGED..."

SO THAT'S WHY THE ALARMS DIDN'T GO OFF!

THE MELTER -- HE MUST HAVE BURNED A SHAFT UP THROUGH THE FOUNDATIONS!

"NOW NORMALLY, THIS GUY WOULDN'T BE A PROBLEM..."

"...EXCEPT HE'S NOT ALONE. SEEMS THAT OUR OLD ENEMY BARON ZEMO HAS PUT TOGETHER A NEW MASTERS OF EVIL..."

"NOT ONLY THAT, ZEMO HAD BROUGHT ALONG A LITTLE INSURANCE - IN THE SHAPE OF A WHITE NOISE GENERATOR..."

"...AND WITH WHIRLWIND AND THE RADIOACTIVE MAN ON BOARD, IT'S ONE HEAVY DUTY OUTFIT."

SKREE QURRRKK KRHHHH

HARD TO CONCENTRATE, AIN'T IT COBBERS?

NOT FOR US THOUGH, 'COS THE BOSS RIGGED US UP SOME SPECIAL EARPLUGS.

"IT WAS A REAL MESS, SPIDER-MAN. THE SONICS WERE DISRUPTING OUR POWERS AND ZEMO'S BOYS WEREN'T HOLDING BACK..."

VENGEANCE WILL BE OURS, AVENGERS...

NOT TO MENTION THE BILLIONS OF DOLLARS WORTH OF STARK TECHNOLOGY CONTAINED IN THIS BUILDING!

FZOHM

"WELL, YOU KNOW US, WE TRIED OUR BEST. BUT THE ODDS WERE STACKED AND WE WERE TAKEN OUT ONE BY ONE..."

NAAARGH!

"...THOUGH SOMEHOW, I MANAGED TO SHRINK DOWN AS I BLACKED OUT, AND I GUESS THEY COULDN'T FIND ME IN THE DEBRIS."

SO THAT QUINJET TAKING OFF WAS ZEMO AND HIS GANG -- AND I'M ASSUMING THEY'VE TAKEN THE OTHERS HOSTAGE.

YEP, ALONG WITH ALL THE GADGETRY AND COMPUTER FILES THEY COULD CARRY. BUT I SWEAR, IF THEY HARM JAN...

CONTINUED ON PAGE 56...

# YELLOWJACKET

Check it out, webheads! Hank Pym has had not one, but four different Super Hero identities! Read on to discover all about his past!

## SPIDEY DATA

**REAL NAME:** DR. HENRY PYM
**OCCUPATION:** BIOCHEMIST AND FULL TIME MEMBER OF THE AVENGERS
**HEIGHT:** 6'
**WEIGHT:** 185 lbs
**POWERS/ABILITIES:** HE CAN CHANGE HIS SIZE USING PYM PARTICLES, MENTALLY CONTROL INSECTS AND HAS THE ABILITY TO FIRE BIO-ELECTRIC BLASTS.

## SMALL SCIENCE!

Early in his career as a biochemist, Dr. Henry 'Hank' Pym discovered an amazing sub-atomic particle that could be used to radically alter a person's size. The first time he used these 'Pym Particles' he shrunk down to just a few millimetres tall, and found himself trapped inside an ant's nest!

## MINI-MARVEL!

After restoring himself to normal size, he designed a helmet that would allow him to control insects. Using this headset and his shrinking powers he became the Super Hero, Ant-Man.

## LARGER THAN LIFE!

A little while later, he discovered a way of using the Pym Particles to make a person grow in size, up to a maximum of 30 feet tall. This discovery led to him becoming the Super Hero Giant-Man, and later on Goliath.

## A NEW HERO!

After years of being Giant-Man, Hank has now decided to scale down his Super Hero plans, and has become Yellowjacket. Like his Ant-Man persona he can shrink and communicate with insects. He also has the ability to fire blasts of bio-energy from his specially constructed gloves.

# TITANIC TEAM-UP!

**As Ant-Man, Hank was one of the founding members of the Avengers!**

He can use Pym Particles to shrink or grow any object!

## WEDDING BELLS!

Hank is married to fellow Avenger Janet Von Dyne, AKA The Wasp.

When Yellowjacket shrinks he still retains his normal strength level making him pint-sized and super strong!

After years of exposure to Pym Particles, Hank now has a special field around his body which allows him to change his size at will!

...CONTINUED FROM PAGE 53!

-- AND RETURN IT IN TRUMPS!

SPA-DANG

UNGH!

THE BATTLE RAGES ON, AND WITH THE MASTERS OF EVIL ON THE VERGE OF DEFEAT...

NO POINT IN SACRIFICING MYSELF TO A LOST CAUSE...

NOT WHEN I CAN ABSCOND WITH THESE PRICELESS AVENGERS' FILES!

HOBGOBLIN'S ESCAPING. THERE'S NO WAY OF CATCHING HIM...

...BUT I'M SURE HAWKEYE WON'T MIND IF I BORROW HIS GEAR A SECOND.

KABOOM

YEP, NOT BAD FOR A NOVICE!

THWIPP

# ANSWERS

## SPIDER-MAN TRUTH TRAIL!

Heads up, Spidey fans! The Green Goblin has kidnapped Mary Jane and I need to get through this maze to find her! Each time you reach a box you need to decide whether the statement is true or false and follow that path. But be careful, guys, if you take the wrong path I'm gonna end up in the clutches of one of these super villains!

**START**

Spider-Man's real name is Peter Parker

Doctor Octopus has 10 robotic arms

The Green Goblin's real name is Norman Osborn

Spider-Man lives in New York

Aunt May is really the Sandman.

The Vulture has a blue costume.

**FINISH**

ANSWERS ON PAGE 62...

28

## PAGE 28
# TRUTH TRAIL!

## PAGE 48
# FANTASTIC FOES!

# FACT ATTACK

THE FALSE FACT ON PAGES 4–5 IS...

Peter Parker is actually scared of heights!

62